The Tea Table

Soups, Savories & Sweets
from the Elmwood Inn

Bruce and Shelley Richardson

Photography by Bruce Richardson

Other books by Bruce & Shelley Richardson:
A Year of Teas at the Elmwood Inn
A Tea for All Seasons
The Great Tea Rooms of Britain
The Great Tea Rooms of America

For information on the complete line of
Elmwood Inn Fine Teas & Gourmet Foods,
or to order autographed copies of the Richardsons' books,
call 1-800-765-2139 or visit our web site at
www.elmwoodinn.com

Copyright ©2003
by Shelley & Bruce Richardson

Photographs copyright ©2003
by Bruce Richardson

Printed in China

BENJAMIN PRESS
A Division of Elmwood Inn
205 East Fourth Street
Perryville, Kentucky 40468 USA
800-765-2139
www.elmwoodinn.com

ISBN 0-966-3478-1-1

The Tea Table

Soups, Savories & Sweets
from the Elmwood Inn

BENJAMIN PRESS

Tea As Ceremony

The clipper ship *Taeping* set a remarkable record at the port of London in 1866. The tall-sail ship, her deep holds filled with chests of tea, delivered her precious cargo from China in an amazing 99 days. It was an impressive feat.

As the exciting news spread across Britain, many thoughtful folks made the comment that the world was moving too fast when you could get tea from China in less than 100 days!

Life has not slowed in the ensuing years. We are often swept up in the frenetic rush to move faster. Like mother birds feeding chirping chicks, we toss French fries to our hungry brood in the back seat of the car as we speed down the road to another sporting event. We impatiently press the elevator "close door" button if we can't bear to wait the four seconds allotted by Mr. Otis to shut the door behind us.

It seems as though the tea world is paddling upstream against an ever-increasing current of time-saving incursions. That may be tea's lasting allure. Why are more and more people turning to the ancient way of tea?

It may be because tea wisely commands our time and attention. We must wait for the kettle to boil. Then the leaf makes us wait another three to five minutes to brew properly. We pour the mystical liquid into a cup and again wait a moment before our lips can drink its refreshment. During this time our breathing quiets. Our pulse returns to normal. We may have a gentle conversation with our family or friends. It is in these moments that our souls are refreshed. We become more human. The cup of serenity performs its magic. Renewed by this ceremony, we hesitate to move back into the fast lane of society's speedway.

Tea is always ceremony. Whether you're preparing a cup of tea simply because you're tired and need a lift, or planning an afternoon tea for 50 guests, there are certain things which remain constant. In true Japanese tradition, the surroundings of the tea ceremony are as important as the tea itself. Here are a few age-old principles that apply to each tea event.

Beauty matters. You, as the host, select the setting, the art, the music, the flowers, the pottery, the silverware, the tea and the foods that appeal to you. You can't please everyone, not even when serving tea. I've discovered that when you please yourself, you are giving of yourself. If we like something and are excited and feel joy, chances are our enthusiasm will be infectious and guests will respond positively.

Shelley and I visited the home of artist Georgia O'Keefe a few years ago. Walking reverently through her adobe home in Abiqu, New Mexico, I spotted on her pantry shelves a couple of jars with fading, hand-printed labels. One read "TEA," the other read "GOOD TEA."

I found it affirming that one of the world's greatest painters shared my love for exceptional tea. I can only hope that, had I been a guest in her home when she was alive, she would have shared the second jar with me.

The second affirmation was that in all of Georgia O'Keefe's personal library of 3,000 books, the volume that she most often asked to be read to her in her last years was *The Book of Tea* by Kakuzo Okakura. The writer's thoughts on art appreciation and the tea room still point us to the wisdom found in a humble cup of tea.

How can you create your unique tea ceremony? Your tea ceremony needs to reflect who you are, what you love, where you have been, where you are going. You may have a beautiful antique English teapot that was given to you by a favorite aunt, teacups that belonged to your mother, silver which you found at an out-of-the-way antique shop on a family vacation, tea given to you by a best friend, roses from your garden, or lace doilies that have been in your family for generations. These items speak to you and, subsequently, to your guests.

Food matters. There is great truth to the adage that we "taste first with our eyes." Food at a tea ceremony is judged by quality rather than quantity.

I can't tell you how many times I've heard callers over the phone say that they "just aren't sure there will be enough to eat" at our afternoon teas. I often think that's like saying, "I don't go to St. So-and-So Church because the communion wafers are small, and they don't give you enough wine." Somehow, they are missing the point.

We celebrate communion because it satisfies a spiritual hunger. The same is true of tea. We celebrate the tea event to feed our souls and not just our stomachs. Society easily can have its hunger pangs cured at the drive-up windows of fast-food restaurants. More often, it is our spirit that needs healing.

Whenever I speak to groups about tea, I always leave time for questions from the audience. There are a number of questions that are common to almost every group. One question is always, "What is high tea?" Since most Americans have their first taste of tea in British-inspired tea houses, I have made a list of the most common tea meals.

High Tea is a term originally used to describe a common British supper, served after 5:30 and accompanied by a pot of tea. The term "high" has nothing to do with the elegance of the meal. Some scholars believe "high" meant that the tea meal was taken at a *high* dining table. This was to distinguish the meal from the fancy afternoon teas taken at *low* tables as you sat on couches in London hotels.

Afternoon Tea, or low tea, is a leisurely afternoon tea meal usually served in fine fashion and in several courses. Afternoon teas are generally more elegant than evening high teas.

Cream Tea is a term for a pot of tea accompanied by scones with clotted cream and preserves. This is a common quick refreshment found in over 2,000 British tea rooms. The term "cream" applies to the clotted cream, or Devon-shire Cream, rather than the action of putting cream in your tea. (Cream is too rich to accompany tea. Milk is the preferred addition.)

Elmwood Inn is unusual in the fact that we have always served only one form of tea meal - afternoon tea. What goes into designing a proper afternoon tea menu? Here's our advice.

♦ An afternoon tea should combine both sweets and savories. Tea sandwiches and/or quiche add balance to a beautiful presentation of small sweets such as shortbread, dipped fruits, cookies, cakes, sorbets or muffins. Of course, you probably will offer scones accompanied by lemon curd, or clotted cream and preserves.

♦ We have always included a cake course. Cakes should not be overly sweet or heavily frosted. Portions should be small if other foods are served. It is much better to serve several small, beautiful foods rather than large portions. After all, the purpose of afternoon tea is to satisfy the soul rather than the stomach!

♦ Food at teatime should be extraordinary. Its appearance should indicate that someone has gone above the call of duty to make each item beautiful - sandwiches neatly trimmed, curled carrots on cucumbers, hand-dipped fruit, tea cakes decorated with garden flowers, golden scones served with strawberry jam in a cut glass dish, water glasses with a thin slice of lemon.

♦ One liberating aspect of owning an American tea room has been that we are free to draw on so many cuisines. We can mix the best of British, French or American dishes. There are no absolutes in putting together a menu. Remember, *if it pleases you, it will please your guests.*

♦ The most important element is the tea. Offer a choice of fresh loose teas made in teapots that hold heat well. There are many fascinating teas to try these days. Half the fun of afternoon tea is discovering a new tea or a delicious blend. Taste the tea first before adding sugar, lemon or milk. Adding something to tea before you taste it is like salting your food before you try it. Pay homage to the tea blender by tasting the unadulterated tea first.

Etiquette matters. Whether we like it or not, there is a degree of protocol and etiquette which accompanies all our activities. Teatime and etiquette have always been married. Whether it was the ancient Chinese tea ceremony, the refined Japanese tea ceremony, or the English afternoon tea ritual, each was accompanied by its own set of rules.

Unfortunately, the English ceremony has been caricatured over the years by a few outlandish ideas which now seem silly, such as sticking your little pinkie out while you hold your cup, or insisting on putting milk into the cup before the tea. I suggest you simply shut off your cell phone and use your best manners while making your guests feel comfortable and relaxed.

Conversation matters. I have had women tell me they have had more conversation with their husbands at an hour-long tea than they had the entire month at home! There is something about tea that encourages our social skills. We recount past meetings in wonderful places or remember stories sparked by pouring tea from a familiar old teapot. Tea and conversation are natural allies. We are quiet. We listen more intently. The pace of life slows and we contemplate beautiful things and savor the company of those who gather with us. All the while, we are building new memories.

Shelley and I hope that this book inspires you to infuse tea into your daily life. Drink it morning, noon and night. Share it with your family and friends. Develop your own tea ceremony. Make it your *cup of serenity* as you nurture your soul.

Bruce Richardson

SOUPS

Beet and Parsnip Soup   *Blueberry Soup*   Cold Melon Soup
Strawberry Soup   Creamy Lemon Soup   *Green and Red Soup*

Beet and Parsnip Soup

*Not quite borscht, this lighter version is a perfect match for high tea.
Served in blue willow stoneware, it is a delight to the eye!*

2 cups chicken broth
3 cups water
1 pound fresh beets, peeled and grated
1 cup fresh parsnips, peeled and grated
2 tablespoons brown sugar
1 large tomato, peeled, cored, and seeded
1 large apple (such as Jonathan or Granny Smith), peeled, cored, seeded
1 tablespoon lemon juice
2 large onions, finely chopped
1 tablespoon red wine vinegar
fresh dill
plain yogurt or sour cream

Combine chicken broth and water in a large soup pot. Bring to a boil. Add beets, parsnips, and sugar. Reduce heat and simmer partially covered for 20 minutes.

Puree tomato and apple in food processor; add to soup mixture. Add lemon juice, onions, and vinegar. Cover and simmer for 20 minutes. Stir in about 1 tablespoon of chopped dill.

After soup has cooled slightly, puree about half in a food processor and return to pot. To serve, garnish each serving with a dollop of yogurt or sour cream. Top with fresh dill or chopped green onion.

Blueberry Soup

This trio of cold summer soups, served in Bruce's collection of antique Aynsley teacups, is a colorful touch of paradise on a hot summer day.

2 cups blueberries
1/4 cup orange juice
dash allspice
dash freshly grated nutmeg
2 cups yogurt
2 thin orange slices
fresh mint

Blend blueberries, orange juice, allspice, and nutmeg in blender or food processor on low speed. Chill, covered, in the refrigerator. When ready to serve, ladle into cups and spoon yogurt into the center of each. Garnish with orange slices and mint.

Cold Melon Soup

1 (2 1/2 to 3 pound) cantaloupe, seeded, peeled and chopped (about three cups)
2-3 tablespoons orange juice
2 teaspoons sugar
edible marigolds (optional)
fresh mint (optional)

Combine the cantaloupe, orange juice, and sugar in a blender. Cover and blend until smooth. Transfer to a covered container until ready to serve. Pour into bowls and garnish with edible flowers such as marigolds.

Strawberry Soup

1 cup fresh strawberries
2 tablespoons sugar
1 cup sour cream
4 tablespoons burgundy or grenadine
1 cup heavy cream

Combine strawberries, sugar, sour cream, grenadine, and cream in a blender. Cover and blend on low speed until thoroughly combined. Chill and serve. Garnish with a dollop of sour cream, thinly sliced strawberries, and fresh mint.

Creamy Lemon Soup

Lemon soup accompanied by gingerbread scones fresh from the oven
— the perfect combination for high tea!

1/3 cup freshly squeezed lemon juice
2 1/2 inches lemon rind strips
3 cups homemade chicken broth
1 1/2 teaspoons cornstarch
2 tablespoons chicken broth
1/2 cup chilled heavy cream
salt to taste
fresh chives for garnish

In a saucepan, combine the lemon juice, lemon rind, and broth. Bring to a boil and boil for five minutes. Discard rind. Stir cornstarch into two tablespoons of chicken broth, then whisk into remaining broth mixture. Cook over moderate heat, continually stirring until thickened. Remove from heat and stir in cream.

Using blender, mix the soup with 1/2 cup crushed ice until smooth. Transfer to a metal bowl. Skim any broth off top. Cover and chill completely.

When ready to serve, season with salt, pour into a beautiful punch bowl, and garnish with chives. Ladle into chilled bowls. This soup also is very good served warm.

Green and Red Soup

This brilliant combination of tastes and colors will certainly delight your guests. Pieces of toasted bread cut into teapot shapes add a whimsical touch to this delicious soup.

Green Soup
2 10-ounce packages frozen peas
6 cups chicken broth
1/4 cup butter, room temperature
1/4 cup all-purpose flour
salt

Combine peas and broth in a two-quart saucepan. Bring to a boil, then lower heat and simmer, covered, for 15 minutes. Cool slightly, then puree in blender and return to saucepan. Combine butter and flour in a small bowl, then add to the peas. Stir over medium heat until soup bubbles and begins to thicken. Season with salt to taste.

Red Soup
1/4 cup butter
1 small onion, minced
1/4 cup all-purpose flour
3 cups half and half
3 cups crushed tomatoes
1/2 teaspoon dried basil
1/2 teaspoon garlic
salt & sugar

Melt butter in a two-quart saucepan over medium heat. Sauté onion for 10 minutes, then sprinkle with flour. Gradually stir in the half-and-half. Keep stirring over medium heat until mixture bubbles and thickens. Stir in tomatoes, basil, garlic, and salt (to taste). Add just a pinch of sugar.

Using two ladles, pour the soups simultaneously into the bowl from both sides. The colors should remain somewhat separated. Garnish with toasted pieces of bread cut with a cookie cutter into any shape desired.

SAVORIES

Apple Chicken Salad in Pastry Shells Cranberry Chicken Salad Tarts *Stuffed Christmas Muffins* Apple Harvest Tea Sandwich *Scallion Biscuits with Ham and Horseradish* Curried Tuna and Apple Tea Sandwich *Apricot, Globe Grape, and Blue Cheese Tea Sandwich* Blue Cheese Tea Sandwich *Mango Chicken Salad in Pastry Shells* Sun Dried Tomato Tea Sandwich *Chicken and Olive Christmas Tea Sandwich* Cucumber with Chevre and Sun Dried Tomato *Curried Spinach Rolls* Cucumber Christmas Surprise Tea Sandwich *Elmwood's Chicken and Watercress Tea Sandwich* Falling Leaves Tea Sandwich *Feta, Lemon and Mint Tea Sandwich* Nutty Carrot Tea Sandwich *Smoked Chicken, Tomato and Spinach Tea Sandwich* Goat Cheese and Watercress Tea Sandwich *Marigold and Curried Egg Salad* Zucchini Relish Pinwheels *Freear's Zucchini Relish* Garden Vegetable Paté Tea Sandwich *Peggy's Perfect Peach and Brie Tea Sandwich* Smoked Turkey and Dried Fruit Paté Tea Sandwich *Blue Cheese and Cranberry Savories* Artichoke and Roasted Red Pepper Savories *Sweet Potato Angel Biscuits with Country Ham* Irish Tea Eggs *Katie's Olive Cheese Balls* Roasted Potatoes on Puff Pastry *Sealed with a Quiche* Smoked Salmon and Chive Tea Tarts *Roast Beef, Apple and Watercress Salad* Spiced Up Chicken Tea Salad *Valentine Tea Party Sandwich* Cucumber Tea Hearts *Strawberry Chicken Salad Tea Sandwich*

Apple Chicken Salad in Pastry Shells

Chicken salad can be found in almost every American tea room. This recipe gives a new look to an old standard. Tiny crisp pastry shells can be purchased in most grocery stores. Keep a supply on hand for quick meals or make your own using our recipe.

Apple Chicken Salad
12 ounces boneless chicken breasts, baked or poached, chopped
1/2 cup finely chopped apple
1/4 cup finely chopped green onion
1/4 cup sour cream
1/4 cup mayonnaise
1 teaspoon coriander
1/2 teaspoon salt
1/8 teaspoon pepper
36 to 40 mini pastry shells, baked
chopped green onion for garnish

Combine first 8 ingredients, stirring well. Cover and chill at least one hour. Prepare pastry shells and fill each one. Garnish with green onions.

Pastry Shells
2 cups all-purpose flour
pinch of salt
1/2 cup shortening
1/2 cup butter, well-chilled
4 to 5 tablespoons cold water

Preheat oven to 450° F. Mix together flour and salt. With a pastry blender, cut butter and shortening into flour until mixture resembles coarse meal. Add cold water a little at a time, until mixture is moist enough to form a ball. Do not over mix. Cover and chill 15 minutes. On a floured surface, roll out pastry with a floured rolling pin. Grease mini-muffin tins. Cut pastry into 3-inch circles and press each circle into a muffin cup. Bake for 8 minutes. Cool completely.

Cranberry Chicken Salad Tarts

We love to incorporate cranberries into our menu at other times than the holidays. The availability of dried cranberries means that these flavorful tarts can be made year-round.

1/2 cup boneless chicken breasts, cooked and diced into small pieces
2 tablespoons celery, finely chopped
2 tablespoons dried cranberries
1/2 teaspoon chopped fresh marjoram leaves (or 1/8 teaspoon dried marjoram may be substituted)
mayonnaise
2 tablespoons chopped pistachio nuts
15 small sprigs marjoram for garnish

<u>Tart Shells</u>
1 1/4 cups all-purpose flour
1/4 teaspoon salt
6 tablespoons unsalted butter, chilled and cut into small pieces
1/4 cup ice water

Place flour and salt in a food processor and pulse on and off to mix. Add butter and pulse machine about 20 times until butter resembles peas. Pour in ice water. Pulse until dough holds together. Remove dough and refrigerate about 1 hour.

Preheat oven to 400° F. Remove dough from refrigerator and pinch into small balls. Pat dough balls into mini-muffin tins or small tart pans. Bake 7-10 minutes, or until light brown. Remove tarts from oven, cool, and set aside.

Mix chicken, cranberries, celery, and chopped marjoram. Moisten with mayonnaise.

Spoon heaping teaspoonful of mixture into each tart shell. Sprinkle with nuts and garnish with marjoram sprigs. Makes about 15 small tarts.

Stuffed Christmas Muffins

The unexpected combination of savory and sweet makes a bite-size treat that is hard to resist. The muffins may be made ahead and kept frozen until ready to use.

3/4 cup milk
1/3 cup vegetable oil
1/4 cup frozen orange juice concentrate, thawed
2 teaspoons grated orange peel
1 egg, slightly beaten
2 1/4 cups all-purpose flour
1/2 cup sugar
3 teaspoons baking powder
1/4 teaspoon salt
1/4 cup sugar
1 1/4 teaspoons grated orange peel

Heat oven to 400° F. Grease bottoms of 36 mini-muffin cups. Beat milk, oil, juice concentrate, 2 teaspoons orange peel and egg in a large bowl with a whisk until blended. Stir together flour, 1/2 cup sugar, baking powder and salt. Add to liquid mixture and stir only until moistened (batter will appear lumpy). Divide batter evenly among muffin cups.

Combine 1/4 cup sugar and orange peel. Sprinkle over batter in cups. Bake 10 to 15 minutes or until light golden brown. Let stand 5 minutes, then remove from pan and cool completely.

<u>Ham Spread</u>
2 cups Virginia baked ham, finely-ground
1/4 cup orange marmalade
1 teaspoon stone ground mustard

Mix ham, orange marmalade and ground mustard to make a chunky spread. Make a vertical cut halfway through the muffin. Stuff with the ham mixture. Garnish with fresh parsley.

Apple Harvest Tea Sandwich

We love to visit the orchards across Central Kentucky during the fall apple harvest. Crisp slices of sweet apple make an extraordinary teatime sandwich.

1 8-ounce package cream cheese, softened
2 tablespoons brown sugar
1/2 teaspoon cinnamon
1/4 teaspoon nutmeg
1 teaspoon vanilla
1 loaf cinnamon-raisin bread
2 Red or Golden Delicious apples, unpeeled
lemon juice
1/3 cup chopped, roasted, and lightly salted peanuts or walnuts

Combine cream cheese, brown sugar, cinnamon, nutmeg, and vanilla. Beat at medium speed with an electric mixer one minute or until smooth. Set aside.

Core apples and slice into thin horizontal slices. Brush with lemon juice.

To assemble a sandwich, spread one side of two slices of bread with cream cheese mixture. Top one slice of bread with apple slices, then place the other piece of bread on top of apples (cream cheese side down). Trim edges. Cut diagonally twice. Lightly spread cheese mixture on front edges. Dip into chopped nuts and serve.

Scallion Biscuits with Ham and Horseradish

Biscuits
2 cups all-purpose flour
2 teaspoons baking powder
1 1/4 teaspoons salt
1/4 teaspoon dry mustard
1/3 cup vegetable shortening
2 large green onions, minced
1 tablespoon fresh parsley, minced
3/4 cup plus 1 1/2 tablespoons milk

Preheat oven to 425° F. In a large bowl, sift together flour, baking powder, salt and dry mustard. With a pastry blender, cut in shortening. Stir in green onions and parsley. Gently stir in enough milk to make a soft dough. Turn onto a lightly floured surface. Pat dough into 3/4-inch thickness and sprinkle lightly with a little flour. With a small biscuit cutter, cut out rounds and place on a lightly greased baking sheet.

Bake about 15 to 18 minutes or until golden brown. Remove from oven and cool for about 10 minutes.

Pickled Onion
1 small red onion, minced
1/4 cup seasoned rice vinegar

Toss the onion and vinegar together and marinate for at least 30 minutes or up to three hours.

Country Ham Mixture
1 1/2 to 2 cups country ham, finely chopped
horseradish sauce - just enough to hold ham together

Split each biscuit in half and spread one half with country ham spread. Top with pickled onions, then replace biscuit top. Arrange on platter and serve immediately. Makes 15 to 18 sandwich biscuits.

Curried Tuna and Apple Tea Sandwich

1 6-ounce can solid white albacore tuna, drained
1/4 cup celery, finely chopped
1/4 cup golden raisins
2 tablespoons diced onion
1 small Braeburn or Gala apple, chopped and tossed in lemon juice
1/2 teaspoon curry powder
1/8 teaspoon garlic powder
1/4 cup light mayonnaise
1 tablespoon lemon juice
24 to 30 diamond-shaped bread pieces (whole wheat preferred)

Mix tuna, celery, raisins, onion and apple together. In a small bowl, whisk together mayonnaise, curry, garlic and lemon juice. Pour dressing over tuna mixture and toss together. Spread mixture on each piece of bread and garnish with small thinly-sliced apple.

Apricot, Globe Grape, and Blue Cheese Tea Sandwich

Large red globe grapes are usually available from fall until mid-January. This recipe makes an easy, colorful sandwich for festive Christmas teas.

3/4 cup garlic and herb spreadable cream cheese
1/4 cup crumbled blue cheese
1/4 cup dried apricots, chopped
24 large red globe grapes
24 pieces of cocktail party rye bread
fresh chives or scallions, chopped

Mix together cream cheese, blue cheese, and apricots. Cut grapes in half and remove any seed particles.

Spread cheese mixture on each slice of bread. Cut in half to make a triangle. Place a grape half, sliced side down, on top of each triangle. Garnish with chives. Makes 48 tea sandwiches which can be prepared and refrigerated up to 6 hours before serving.

Blue Cheese Tea Sandwich

We always love recipes that can be made well ahead. The ingredients for this sandwich can be made weeks in advance.

Blue Cheese Spread
1 8-ounce package cream cheese, softened
1 4-ounce package blue cheese
pecan halves for garnish
red and yellow peppers for garnish

Mix two cheeses together, either in a food processor or with hand mixer. Store in plastic container in refrigerator until ready to use.

Crackers
3/4 cup all-purpose flour
3/4 cup toasted pecans, finely ground
4 tablespoons butter, cut into small pieces
1/3 cup blue cheese, crumbled

Combine flour and pecans in food processor. Pulse to combine. Add butter and pulse until mixture resembles coarse meal. Add blue cheese and process until dough is completely combined. Transfer dough to work surface and shape into a 2-inch wide log. Wrap in plastic wrap and refrigerate 24 hours. (Dough may be kept in the refrigerator for up to 2 weeks and in the freezer up to 4 weeks.)

Heat oven to 325° F. Slice chilled log into 1/4 inch thick slices. Place slices on a baking sheet and bake. Rotate the baking sheet about halfway through cooking. Bake 25 to 35 minutes or until the crackers are golden brown and firm in the center. Transfer to cooling rack, then to an airtight container when totally cooled. May be kept at room temperature.

To assemble a sandwich, spread about a teaspoon of spread on each cracker. Garnish with a thin strip of red and yellow pepper placed on top of spread, crisscrossing. Place a toasted pecan half in the center of the peppers. Serve immediately.

Mango Chicken Salad in Pastry Shells

Mango is one of those versatile fruits that mixes well with chicken or even with hot or iced tea. This recipe will serve a large tea party.

3 cups diced cooked chicken (chicken may be poached or baked)
1 cup finely chopped celery
1/4 cup finely chopped scallions
2 mangoes, peeled and cut into small pieces
3 tablespoons lemon juice

<u>Dressing</u>
1/3 cup plain yogurt
1/3 cup mayonnaise
2 3/4 teaspoons curry powder
1/2 teaspoon cumin
salt and pepper, to taste
1 cup cashews, roasted and chopped
2 tablespoons fresh chopped cilantro
whole cilantro leaves for garnish

In a medium bowl, toss the chicken, celery, scallions, and mangoes with lemon juice. Using a whisk, mix yogurt, mayonnaise, curry and cumin together. Add this dressing to chicken salad, then season with salt and pepper. Chill until ready to serve. Add cashews and cilantro.

Spoon into individual pastry shells and garnish with whole cilantro leaves. This salad also may be served on lettuce leaves. Serves 6 to 8 using medium pastry shells or about 24 using miniature shells.

Sun Dried Tomato Tea Sandwich

The rich combination of sun dried tomatoes, pine nuts and roasted red peppers makes a satisfying paste that can be made ahead and refrigerated until ready to spread on a hearty bread.

<u>Spread</u>
1 cup oil-packed sun dried tomatoes, drained
1 jar (12 ounces) roasted sweet red peppers, drained
1 cup packed fresh basil leaves
1/2 cup pine nuts, toasted
1 tablespoon olive oil
1 tablespoon balsamic vinegar
2 large garlic cloves
1 1/2 teaspoons grated lemon peel
1 loaf rye or black olive bread

Chop all ingredients in a food processor to make a coarse paste. Season with salt and pepper. Spread on slice of bread. Top with another slice. Trim all edges, then slice diagonally twice, making four triangle sandwiches.

Chicken and Olive Christmas Tea Sandwich

*This is one of the easiest chicken salad sandwiches you will ever make.
The addition of olive slices gives each sandwich a colorful look.*

9 ounces cooked chicken breasts, diced
1/2 cup green pimento-stuffed olives, drained and thinly sliced
1/3 cup pimentos, drained and sliced
1/4 cup sour cream
4 medium green onions, finely chopped
1 loaf good sandwich bread, frozen, and cut into 40 2-inch rounds

Combine chicken, olives, pimentos, and green onions in medium mixing
bowl. Moisten with sour cream until mixture is spreadable. Using a
spreading knife, cover each frozen bread round with one tablespoon of
chicken mixture. Garnish with two or three olive slices. Sandwiches may
be made ahead up to 24 hours in advance and stored in airtight
container.

Cucumber with Chevre and Sun Dried Tomato

Most people think cucumbers can only be found on sandwiches at tea time. This attractive combination of cheese and crisp cucumber slices should be kept chilled until ready to serve.

1 large English cucumber (seedless)
1/2 cup sun dried tomato paste
8 ounces cream cheese
1 cup crumbled chevre
32 small fresh basil leaves

Make indentions lengthwise down body of cucumber with tines of fork. Cut cucumber into about 32 slices, 1/2-inch thick. Place on a paper towel to drain.

Combine sun dried tomato paste and cream cheese in processor. Spoon mixture into a pastry bag, then pipe about one teaspoon on each cucumber slice. Sprinkle with 1/2 teaspoon chevre. Garnish with a small basil leaf and place on ice chips or a small piece of leaf lettuce to serve.

Curried Spinach Rolls

We love to work unusual ingredients into our tea recipes. No one expects to have spinach at a tea. Most guests eat these delicious rolls and then ask what the secret ingredient was.

1 teaspoon curry powder
1/2 teaspoon ground cumin
8 ounces cream cheese
4 ounces feta cheese
3 cups fresh chopped spinach
2 garlic cloves, minced
4 ounces roasted red pepper
1 tablespoon finely chopped crispy bacon
1/4 teaspoon hot pepper sauce
chopped parsley or cilantro
1 loaf dark pumpernickel bread

Stir curry and cumin in a small dry skillet over medium heat until fragrant, about 45 seconds. Remove from heat.

Combine cream cheese, feta cheese, spinach, garlic, and roasted red pepper in a food processor. Blend until pureed. Add curry mixture, bacon and hot sauce. Blend once again. Season to taste with salt and pepper, then transfer to a covered container and refrigerate.

To assemble, remove crusts from bread with a sharp bread knife. Flatten squares of bread with a rolling pin. Spread curry mixture on top of each slice of bread, then roll into a log.

Cut bread diagonally; each log should make approximately three sandwiches. Dip end of sandwich rolls into chopped parsley to garnish. Makes about 48-60 rolls.

Cucumber Christmas Surprise Tea Sandwich

The surprise in this sandwich is the addition of crisp pea pods. Who knew tea time recipes could be so healthy!

1/2 cup fresh snow pea pods, trimmed
4 slices dark rye sandwich bread
4 slices white sandwich bread
3 or 4 ounces soft chevre, rolled in cracked black pepper
1/3 cup roasted soy nuts (lightly salted or seasoned)
1/2 English seedless cucumber, thinly sliced
1 medium tomato, thinly sliced
salt

Cook the pea pods in lightly salted boiling water for about 2 minutes. Rinse with cold water. Drain. Place in a small bowl and chill. Spread chevre on one side of each slice of bread. Sprinkle four slices of white bread with soy nuts, gently pressing nuts into the cheese.

Place about four cucumber slices on top of nuts. Open the pea pods and place two or three on top of cucumber, then follow with tomato slices. Top with a slice of rye bread. Trim edges and cut into triangles with a serrated knife. Makes 16 finger sandwiches.

Elmwood's Chicken and Watercress Tea Sandwich

Watercress is one of the great ingredients for tea sandwiches. This recipe is one of the most requested at Elmwood Inn.

4 boneless chicken breasts, roasted and chopped
1 teaspoon curry powder
1/3 cup mayonnaise
1 teaspoon chopped fresh chives
1 teaspoon chopped fresh tarragon
salt to taste
1/8 teaspoon freshly ground pepper
1 bunch watercress, stemmed
16 slices hearty country white bread
1 cup toasted pistachios, finely chopped

In a medium bowl, combine mayonnaise, curry powder, chives, tarragon, salt and pepper. Mix well and stir in chicken. If necessary, add a little more mayonnaise.

Chutney Butter
6 tablespoons unsalted butter, softened
1 tablespoon coarse grain mustard
1 tablespoon mango chutney, finely chopped

Beat butter, mustard, and chutney together until well blended.

To assemble sandwiches, spread one slice of bread with chutney butter. Top with chicken filling and layer with watercress leaves. Butter another slice of bread and top sandwich, butter side down.

Remove crusts with a sharp bread knife and cut into three fingers. Thinly spread mayonnaise onto one or two sides of sandwich fingers and dip into chopped pistachios. Cover and refrigerate until ready to serve. Makes about 24 sandwich fingers.

Falling Leaves Tea Sandwich

The colors and textures of autumn burst forth in this brilliant sandwich.
This is a great way to work healthful vegetables into afternoon tea.

Beet Mixture
1 16-ounce jar Harvard beets
6 ounces cream cheese
1 garlic clove, minced
pinch of sugar
1/2 cup Gorgonzola cheese, crumbled
1/3 cup toasted and ground walnuts

In a food processor, blend the beets, cream cheese, garlic, sugar, and Gorgonzola. Add ground walnuts at the end just to blend. Place mixture in storage container.

Carrot Mixture
1 15-ounce jar baby carrots, drained
1 8-ounce package cream cheese
2 green onions, minced
1 loaf hearty white sandwich bread
1 loaf hearty dark wheat sandwich bread

In a food processor, blend the carrots, cream cheese, and green onions until spreadable. Salt to taste. Place mixture in a storage container.

To assemble sandwiches, spread one piece of white bread with beet mixture and another piece of white bread with carrot mixture. Place a slice of dark wheat bread between the two fillings. Trim the crusts and slice into 3 finger sandwiches.

Feta, Lemon and Mint Tea Sandwich

The combination of feta cheese and mint gives our guests a taste of the Mediterranean in this open-faced tea sandwich.

8 ounces feta cheese
2 tablespoons fresh mint, chopped
2 tablespoons lemon juice
1 tablespoon lemon zest
1 loaf dark pumpernickel bread

In a medium bowl, mix together feta cheese, fresh mint, lemon juice, and zest. Set aside or refrigerate until ready to use.

Cut out daisy shapes from pumpernickel. Spread 1-2 tablespoons of the cheese mixture on top of each cut out. Garnish with fresh violets and mint leaves. (Pansies also may be used if violets are not available.)

Makes about 48 open-face sandwiches.

Nutty Carrot Tea Sandwich

1 8-ounce package cream cheese, softened
1/2 teaspoon grated orange rind
1 cup shredded carrots
3/4 cup shredded sharp cheddar cheese
1/2 cup chopped toasted pecans
1/4 cup raisins
1 loaf raisin bread
fresh parsley for garnish

Combine cream cheese and orange rind in a medium bowl. Beat at medium speed with an electric mixer until blended. Stir in carrots, cheddar cheese, pecans, and raisins. Cover and chill until ready to make sandwiches. Makes 2 cups.

To assemble sandwiches, cut out desired shapes from raisin bread. Spread carrot mixture on each piece of bread and garnish with fresh parsley and carrot curls.

Smoked Chicken, Tomato and Spinach Tea Sandwich

4 grilled or smoked chicken breasts, chopped
1/4 cup bacon, cooked and crumbled
fresh spinach leaves
1 loaf hearty white or wheat bread

Dressing
2 tablespoons red wine vinegar
2 tablespoons fresh lemon juice
3/4 cup olive oil
1/2 cup oil-packed sun dried tomatoes, drained and chopped
1/4 cup chopped shallots

Combine chicken and bacon. In a small bowl, whisk together the vinegar, lemon juice, and olive oil. Add the tomatoes and shallots. Set aside. Place several spinach leaves on top of a piece of bread. Top spinach with chicken mixture, then another piece of bread. Trim crusts, then cut diagonally twice, making four triangles. The sides of the sandwich will be colorful with the spinach and tomatoes showing. Makes 40 sandwiches.

Goat Cheese and Watercress Tea Sandwich

11 ounces fresh goat cheese
3/4 cup chopped watercress leaves
16 slices cinnamon-raisin bread
1 cup toasted and finely chopped pecans
soft cream cheese for spreading

In a medium bowl, mix together goat cheese and watercress. Add a little salt for seasoning. Spread mixture evenly over 8 slices of bread. Top with remaining pieces of bread. Cut away all of the crusts and discard. Cut sandwiches diagonally in half and spread soft cream cheese thinly over two sides of sandwich. Place pecans on a flat plate and dip the two sides into the pecans to coat. Cover sandwiches tightly and chill until ready to serve.

Marigold and Curried Egg Salad

Marigold blossoms are prevalent in the gardens at Elmwood Inn. We love to share them with our guests by garnishing these delicious tea sandwiches.

12 hard boiled eggs
1/3 cup mayonnaise
1 tablespoon peach chutney
1 tablespoon Dijon mustard
1 tablespoon curry powder
2 tablespoons golden raisins
1 loaf raisin bread
fresh marigolds for garnish

Finely chop eggs. Place in a large mixing bowl and add mayonnaise, chutney, mustard, curry powder, and raisins. Mix together. Refrigerate until ready to use.

Cut rounds from slices of bread and top each round with the egg salad. Garnish with fresh marigold petals.

Zucchini Relish Pinwheels

6 tortillas
2 cups baked ham, finely ground
3/4 cup zucchini relish
8 ounces cream cheese
1-2 tablespoons mayonnaise (to make a spreadable consistency)
2 cups chopped lettuce
1/4 cup fresh cilantro or dill

In a medium bowl, mix ham, zucchini relish, cream cheese and mayonnaise together. Spread 3-4 tablespoons evenly and completely over each tortilla. Sprinkle chopped lettuce and cilantro on top of the spread. Roll the tortilla up, slice off the end and discard. Cut slices or pinwheels about 2" thick. Arrange on a platter with the inside showing.

Freear's Zucchini Relish

Our office manager, Freear Williams, adapted this recipe from an original recipe by Louise Smart, who once ran the General Store in Perryville.

10 cups ground zucchini
4-5 cups ground onions
5 tablespoons canning salt

Put in large nonmetal bowl and mix well. Let stand overnight. Drain and rinse well (2-3 times). Put in large kettle with the following ingredients:

2 1/4 cups white vinegar
4 1/2 cups sugar
1 tablespoon nutmeg
1 tablespoon dry mustard
1 tablespoon turmeric
1 tablespoon cornstarch
1/2 teaspoon black pepper
2 teaspoons celery salt
2 large sweet green bell peppers, chopped medium
2 large sweet red bell peppers, chopped medium

Bring to a boil, stirring occasionally, for 30 minutes. Pour into 6-8 hot sterilized pint jars and seal. Tighten lids and process in a boiling water bath for 5 minutes.

Garden Vegetable Paté Tea Sandwich

This recipe was inspired from a recipe found in "Splendor in the Bluegrass," a wonderful collection of regional recipes published by the Louisville Junior League.

16 ounces reduced-fat cream cheese, softened
3/4 cup nonfat sour cream
2 tablespoons flour
4 eggs
2 garlic cloves, minced
2 tablespoons lemon juice
1 teaspoon salt
1 teaspoon chili powder
1/2 teaspoon pepper
1/4 teaspoon paprika
1/4 teaspoon hot sauce
1 cup shredded cheddar cheese
1/2 cup finely chopped carrots
1/4 cup finely chopped broccoli
1/4 cup finely chopped green onions
1 cup chopped fresh tomato
2 tablespoons chopped fresh parsley
2 tablespoons chopped fresh chives
1 loaf party rye

Combine cream cheese, sour cream and flour in mixing bowl and beat until blended, scraping the bowl occasionally. Add eggs, one at a time, beating well after each addition. Add garlic, lemon juice, salt, chili powder, pepper, paprika, and hot sauce. Mix well. Fold in cheddar cheese, carrot, broccoli, and green onions.

Spoon vegetable mixture into a greased 9-inch springform pan. Bake at 375° F for 35 to 45 minutes or until set. Cool in pan on a wire rack. Remove side of pan. Chill, covered, in refrigerator until ready to serve.

To prepare tea sandwich, diagonally cut each piece of party rye in half. Spread about a tablespoon of paté on top and garnish with tomato, parsley and chives. Serve immediately.

Peggy's Perfect Peach and Brie Tea Sandwich

This recipe was developed by our kitchen manager, Peggy Powell. The marriage of brie and peaches is accented by the addition of raspberry vinegar.

1/2 cup peach preserves
1 fresh peach, peeled and sliced in small quarters
1 tablespoon minced green onion
1 teaspoon raspberry vinegar
1/8 teaspoon red pepper flakes
1 package party-size French bread
1 medium round of brie
fresh chopped chives

Combine preserves, green onion, raspberry vinegar, and pepper flakes. Set aside. Preheat oven to 350° F. Cut bread slices in half. Place on a cookie sheet and bake until toasted, but not brown. Remove and cool.

To assemble, spread each slice of bread with brie. Place a slice of fresh peach on top of brie and top with preserves mixture. Garnish with fresh chives.

Smoked Turkey and Dried Fruit Paté Tea Sandwich

Here's another easy spread that can be made in advance so that your tea time can be more relaxing. It combines a mouth-watering array of flavors.

1 cup smoked turkey breast, cooked and diced
2 green onions, sliced
1/4 cup softened cream cheese
1/4 cup sour cream
2 tablespoons honey
1/8 teaspoon ground allspice
1/2 cup chopped dried Calimyrna figs
1/2 cup chopped dried apricots
1/4 cup dried cranberries
1/4 cup chopped and toasted pecans
cocktail rye slices

Place the turkey and onions in a food processor. Process until coarsely chopped. Add cream cheese, sour cream, honey and allspice. Cover and process using on and off motions until mixed. Add figs, apricots, cranberries, and pecans. Mix once again using quick on and off motions until fruit is chopped. Do not over process. Remove paté to a bowl. Spread on slices of cocktail rye and slice diagonally. Garnish with chopped parsley and chopped dried cranberries.

Blue Cheese and Cranberry Savories

<u>Crust</u>
1 cup flour
2/3 cup ground walnuts
1 tablespoon sugar
1/4 teaspoon salt
1/2 teaspoon dry mustard
3 ounces cold unsalted butter, cut in cubes
1 to 2 tablespoons milk

In a food processor, pulse the dry ingredients and butter until mixture appears like crumbs. Add milk and pulse until a dough forms. Press dough into a ball and press into a 9-inch tart pan. Prick with a fork, then freeze for about half an hour. Bake at 375° F for 15 minutes or until golden.

<u>Filling</u>
2 tablespoons olive oil
1 large onion, finely diced
1/2 teaspoon salt
1 1/2 cups cranberries, fresh or frozen
1 tablespoon sugar (optional)
2 teaspoons fresh thyme, minced
2 eggs
1 cup heavy cream
3 ounces crumbled blue cheese

Heat olive oil in heavy saucepan over medium heat. Add onions and salt and sauté 10 to 15 minutes. Add cranberries and sugar, cooking until cranberries begin to pop. Stir in thyme and set aside.

In a mixing bowl, combine the eggs and cream, whisking until smooth. Spoon cranberry mixture into baked tart shell, crumbling blue cheese on top. Pour egg mixture over filling. Bake at 350° F until golden brown (about 15-20 minutes). Cool before serving, then cut into wedges.

Artichoke and Roasted Red Pepper Savories

Savory tartlets hold a traditional position on the Elmwood tea menu. We are always looking for new ingredients to add to the basic tartlet recipe. The addition of artichokes and green onions makes this one of our favorite combinations. The savories are pictured on page 40

frozen tart shells or favorite pastry dough
6 eggs
3 cups half-and-half
1/2 teaspoon salt
1/4 teaspoon pepper
1 1/2 cups Asiago cheese, grated
14 ounces artichoke hearts, drained and chopped
7 ounces roasted red pepper, drained and chopped
1/4 cup green onion, chopped or cut into small strips
1/2 cup grated parmesan cheese

Preheat oven to 400° F and partially bake pastry shells before filling (about five minutes). Remove from oven. Reset oven to 350° F.

In a large bowl, whisk eggs, half-and-half, salt and pepper together. Sprinkle a heaping tablespoon of Asiago cheese on the bottom of each tart shell. Top with another heaping tablespoon of artichoke, and then roasted red pepper. Pour egg mixture over the cheese, artichokes, and pepper. Sprinkle parmesan and green onions on top of each tart.

Bake 45 minutes or until golden brown or set. Makes about 8 tarts.

Sweet Potato Angel Biscuits with Country Ham

The heavenly aroma of Angel Biscuits baking in the oven welcomes our guests as they arrive for tea in the fall. The addition of country ham makes these savories irresistible.

3 large sweet potatoes or 3 cups canned mashed sweet potatoes
3 packages active dry yeast
3/4 cup warm water (105-115°)
7 1/2 cups all-purpose flour
1 1/2 cups sugar
1 tablespoon baking powder
1 tablespoon salt
1 1/2 cups shortening

Wash the sweet potatoes and bake at 400° F for one hour or until done. Cool, peel, and mash. Set aside three cups. Combine water and yeast.

Combine flour, sugar, baking powder, and salt. Cut in shortening with a pastry blender until mixture resembles crumbs. Add sweet potatoes and yeast mixture. Stir until dry ingredients are moistened. Turn dough onto a lightly floured surface. Knead 5 minutes. Place dough in a lightly greased bowl. Turn over once to grease top. Cover and refrigerate 8 hours or overnight.

Roll dough out to 1/2 inch thickness. Cut with a 2-inch round cutter. Place on ungreased baking sheets. Cover and allow biscuits to rise in a warm place for 20 minutes or until double. Bake at 400° F for 10-12 minutes or until lightly brown. To serve, split and stuff with country ham.

Irish Tea Eggs

Ireland has the highest per capita tea consumption of any western country. The tannins of robust Irish Blend Tea give these hard-boiled eggs the mottled look of giant marbles.

12 small to medium eggs

Place eggs in a large pan and cover with cold water. Bring to boil over high heat, then reduce to low, simmering uncovered for ten minutes. Drain, cool in cold water, then drain once again. Lightly crack the shells on a hard surface, but do not remove shells.

In a large pan, place:
8 cups water
1/3 cup Elmwood Inn Irish Blend Tea
4 slices fresh ginger, peeled and smashed flat
peel of one orange
1 3-inch cinnamon stick
1 teaspoon salt
fresh chives

Bring all ingredients to boil, reduce to low boil and simmer uncovered about fifteen minutes. Add cracked eggs and continue to simmer for ten minutes. Remove from heat and cool completely in tea mixture.

Remove eggs from liquid and peel. Slice into halves and garnish with a fresh chive sprig. Serve at room temperature or chilled.

Katie's Olive Cheese Balls

Our friends, Katie and Albin Whitworth are master hosts in Lexington, Kentucky. For years, we have enjoyed these savory appetizers as a prelude to their exquisite dinner parties. These savories are equally at home on the tea tray.

2 cups grated sharp cheddar cheese
1/2 cup soft butter
1 1/4 cups flour
1/2 teaspoon salt
1 teaspoon paprika
green stuffed olives, drained

Preheat oven to 400° F. Combine all ingredients except olives. Pinch off a small amount of dough and form into a 1-inch ball. Press an olive into the center of the dough ball. Wrap mixture around olive. Be sure the olive is completely covered. Place on an ungreased cookie sheet. Bake 10-12 minutes. These freeze well unbaked.

Roasted Potatoes on Puff Pastry

This is one of our most requested recipes. The satisfying blend of potatoes, walnuts and cream cheese is highlighted by the intensity of the Gorgonzola cheese.

1 sheet puff pastry
10 small red potatoes, about 2 inches in diameter
1 tablespoon olive oil
1/4 teaspoon salt
1/8 teaspoon pepper
1 4-ounce package cream cheese
2 tablespoons chopped green onion
2 tablespoons chopped chives
1 cup crumbled Gorgonzola cheese
1/2 cup chopped walnuts
chopped chives for garnish

Preheat oven to 400° F. Cut out 10 to 12 rounds of puff pastry with a 2-3 inch cookie cutter and bake on ungreased baking sheet for 10 minutes. Cool, then cut the rounds in halves or thirds to make smaller, flatter puffs. Set aside until ready to use.

Slice off each end of each potato. Discard. Cut potato into 3/8-inch slices (about 3 slices per potato). In a medium bowl, combine potato slices and oil. Toss to coat. Arrange slices on an ungreased cookie sheet. Sprinkle with salt and pepper. Bake for 20 minutes or until tender.

In a small bowl, combine Gorgonzola cheese and walnuts. Mix well. Set aside. In another small bowl, mix together cream cheese, chopped green onions, and chopped chives.

To assemble, take one puff pastry round, spread with a thin layer of the cream cheese mixture. Top with a potato slice, then spread with another thin layer of cream cheese. Top with about 1 tablespoon Gorgonzola cheese and walnut mixture. Garnish with fresh chopped chives or parsley.

May be served warm or at room temperature. Makes about 30.

Sealed with a Quiche

This is a perfect addition to a February Valentine tea. The savory mix of potatoes, bacon and cheese also makes a satisfying one-dish breakfast meal.

Quiche
1 cup very thinly sliced peeled potatoes
1 cup 1/2-inch pieces fresh asparagus
1 cup diced Canadian bacon
1 1/2 cups shredded Havarti cheese
4 eggs
1 cup milk
1/2 teaspoon dried marjoram leaves
1/4 teaspoon salt

Pastry Crust
1 1/2 cups flour
1/2 teaspoon salt
2 tablespoons butter
1/3 cup shortening
2-3 tablespoons cold water

Mix together flour and salt. Cut in shortening and butter until coarse crumbs form. Sprinkle in water while mixing lightly. Form dough into a ball and chill before rolling out.

Heat oven to 400° F. Roll out the pie crust to fit a 9-inch pie plate. Bake about 7 to 8 minutes or until light brown. Layer potatoes, asparagus, bacon and cheese in the partially baked crust. Beat eggs, milk, marjoram and salt until well blended. Pour over mixture in the pie plate. Turn oven down to 350° F. Bake 45 to 50 minutes or until knife inserted in center comes out clean. Let stand for 10 minutes before cutting and serving.

Smoked Salmon and Chive Tea Tarts

1 8-ounce package cream cheese
2 tablespoons minced green onion
2 tablespoons minced fresh chives
1 4.5-ounce package smoked salmon, skin removed, chopped
2 tablespoons mayonnaise
1/8 teaspoon hot pepper sauce
24 small pastry tart shells
chopped fresh chives for garnish

Combine all ingredients except pastry shells and chopped chives in food processor. Mix well. Pipe about a tablespoon of the mixture into each pastry shell. Garnish with chopped chives when ready to serve.

Roast Beef, Apple and Watercress Salad

This recipe is very versatile. It can be used as a salad, served as an appetizer in a pastry cup, or included in an elegant open-faced tea sandwich.

1/2 cup plain, low-fat yogurt
2 tablespoons horseradish sauce
1 1/2 teaspoons lime juice
1/2 teaspoon freshly ground pepper
2 Braeburn or Gala apples, cored, diced, and coated with
one tablespoon lemon juice
1 pound red new potatoes, cooked and diced
1 bunch watercress, slightly chopped (about 4 cups)*
12 to 16 ounces lean roast beef, cooked and coarsely chopped+
minced chives for garnish

Combine yogurt, horseradish sauce, lime juice, and pepper in large bowl. Add apples and potatoes. Toss gently. Add watercress and chopped roast beef. Toss mixture together gently.

For salad, line a salad bowl or plate with extra watercress or spinach leaves. Place salad on top of greens, and garnish with chives.

For appetizers, spoon a heaping tablespoonful into prepared mini pastry cups and garnish.

For tea sandwiches, cut good quality whole grain bread into crustless triangles. Spread with horseradish sauce. Top with watercress sprigs and salad mixture. Garnish with thinly sliced apples and pieces of chives.

*If watercress is unavailable, fresh, spinach leaves may be substituted.

+We cook our roast beef for six to eight hours on low in a crockpot.

Spiced Up Chicken Tea Salad

This adaptable chicken salad can also be served in small pastry shells on a tea tray.

<u>Dressing</u>
1/4 cup sherry wine vinegar
3 tablespoons Dijon mustard
1 1/2 tablespoons ground cumin
1 tablespoon curry powder
1/2 cup olive oil

In a medium bowl, whisk the vinegar, mustard, cumin, and curry together. Add olive oil and whisk to blend. Cover and refrigerate until ready to use. Whisk again at room temperature before using.

<u>Salad</u>
1 cup plain yogurt
1 1/2 teaspoons ground cumin
1 1/2 teaspoons ground coriander
1 teaspoon freshly ground pepper
1 teaspoon ground cardamon
1/2 teaspoon ground cloves
1/2 teaspoon ground cinnamon
2 teaspoons fresh lemon juice
4 large skinless, boneless chicken breasts
8 cups fresh mixed salad greens
1/2 red onion, thinly sliced

In a large bowl, whisk first eight ingredients together. Add the chicken breasts and toss to coat. Cover and refrigerate at least 1 hour or up to a day, turning occasionally.

Prepare barbecue. Grill at medium heat for 20 to 25 minutes (10 to 12 minutes on each side). Juices should run clear when pierced. Remove from grill, cool and chop into bite size pieces or thin strips. Place salad greens in a large salad bowl, add chicken and toss. Add dressing and toss once again. Garnish with sliced red onion.

Valentine Tea Party Sandwich

1 pound baked ham
1/4 cup celery
1/4 cup green onion
2 tablespoons mayonnaise
orange marmalade or chutney
paprika
1 15-ounce can sliced beets
48 slices light whole wheat bread cut into 2-inch rounds

In food processor, chop ham, celery, and green onion. Add mayonnaise to bind mixture and make it spreadable. Refrigerate until ready to use.

Spread one round piece of bread with ham mixture. Spread orange marmalade on the other round piece of bread and place on top of ham side, making a closed sandwich. Pour several tablespoons of paprika onto a sheet of wax paper. Turn sandwich on its side and roll completely around to coat the side of the sandwich. To garnish, drain beets and pat dry. With a one-inch heart cutter, cut a small heart from each beet slice. Place a small beet heart on top of each round sandwich. Makes 48.

Cucumber Tea Hearts

1 8-ounce package cream cheese
1 8-ounce jar Harvard beets
1 tablespoon chopped green onion
1/8 teaspoon ground red pepper
1/8 teaspoon hot sauce
48 slices of white bread
1 cucumber sliced into thin rounds, then quartered

In a food processor, combine cream cheese, beets, green onion, red pepper and hot sauce. Refrigerate until ready to use.

Cut bread into hearts using a 2 or 3-inch cutter. Bread may be frozen at this point until ready to use. Spread bread hearts with filling. Garnish with cucumber quarters, spreading diagonally across sandwich. Makes 48.

Strawberry Chicken Salad Tea Sandwich

Freshly ripened strawberries give a colorful look, delightful aroma, and sweet taste to this springtime sandwich.

4 boneless chicken breasts, roasted or poached, diced
4 green onions, chopped
1 cup cashews, roasted and chopped
1/4 cup sesame seeds, toasted
2 cups fresh strawberries, cut into pieces
1 head red leaf lettuce, washed and crisp
1 loaf sweet Hawaiian bread

Dressing
2 tablespoons sugar
2 teaspoons salt
1/2 teaspoon pepper
4 tablespoons balsamic vinegar
1/2 cup olive oil

In a salad dressing cruet, combine the dressing ingredients and shake vigorously. Put aside.

In a large bowl, combine chicken, onions, cashews, sesame seeds, and strawberries. Toss. Add enough dressing to coat well, then toss again. Spread the chunky salad spread over a slice of bread, top with a piece of lettuce, then another slice of bread. With a sharp bread knife, trim all crusts, then cut diagonally twice, making four triangles. Makes 48-50 tea sandwiches.

SWEETS

Ginger Shortbread Blueberry Curd *Blueberry Streusel Tea Cake with Blueberry Curd* Callie's Christmas Cake *Chocolate Buttermilk Mocha Pound Cake* Carrot-Pineapple Tea Cake *Chocolate Zucchini Cake* Elmwood's Derby Cake *Harvest Moon Cake with Orange Sauce* Irish Cream and Coffee Poundcake *Painted Lady Butterfly Tea Cake* Strawberry Tea Cake *Chocolate Cherry Christmas Bars* Chocolate-Covered Cherry Cookies *Elmwood Macaroons* Chocolate Orange Mousse Tarts *Fruit and Ricotta Tarts* Fruited Oatmeal Tea Cakes *Chocolate Creme de Menthe Bars* Snow Bars *Elmwood Lemon Squares* Iced Cinnamon Apple Oatmeal Tea Cookies *Orange Coconut Sorbet* Gingerbread Scones *Watermelon Sorbet* Chocolate Mousse Halloween Tarts *Frozen Passion Sorbet* Ginger Pear Sorbet *End of the Rainbow Sorbet* Mint Julep Sorbet *Petite White Chocolate Mousse Tarts* Raspberry and Cardamon Cake Trifle *Kentucky Christmas Balls* Chocolate Hazelnut Truffles *Key Lime Coconut Truffles* Raspberry Truffles *Sticky Toffee Tea Cookies* Strawberries with Mascarpone *Rosemary Shortbread* Sweet Summer Iced Tea

Ginger Shortbread

Shortbread is one of the quintessential items found on afternoon tea trays. This recipe incorporates two additional ingredients - candied ginger and chocolate. It is shown here with Petite Chocolate Mousse Tarts. Both recipes come from our longtime friend and co-worker, Jan Sheffield.

1 cup all-purpose flour
1/2 cup unsalted butter, chilled and cut into small pieces
1/3 cup brown sugar
1/4 cup candied ginger, minced
2 tablespoons cornstarch
a pinch of salt

Heat oven to 350° F. Line 8-inch square baking dish with a single piece of aluminum foil, folding excess over the sides. Lightly butter only the bottom of baking dish. Line a cookie sheet with waxed paper and set aside.

Combine flour, butter, brown sugar, ginger, cornstarch and salt in food processor. Whirl until ingredients come together, about 20 seconds. (Stop before mixture forms a ball.) Press mixture evenly into prepared baking dish, and prick all over with a fork. Using fork tines, score lines to form 25 squares. Bake until very light brown around the edges (about 25 minutes). Remove from oven and go over scored lines again with fork. Let cool 10 minutes. Remove from pan, lifting foil ends gently. Cut into 25 squares with a serrated knife. Let cool.

Glaze
4 ounces semi-sweet baking chocolate
1 tablespoon vegetable shortening

When shortbread has cooled, melt chocolate and vegetable shortening in double-boiler; stir well. Dip cookies diagonally into chocolate and place on waxed paper-lined cookie sheet. Refrigerate until firm.

Blueberry Curd

4 cups fresh blueberries, slightly crushed
1/2 cup fresh lemon juice
1 cup sugar
4 eggs (beaten)
1/2 cup unsalted butter
1 tablespoon lemon zest

In a heavy pan, combine berries, lemon juice, sugar, and eggs. Stir constantly over medium heat until blueberries are very soft. Next, add pieces of butter and the zest slowly, stirring constantly over medium heat until mixture just starts to boil. Immediately remove from heat. Cool. Pour into a covered container and place in refrigerator until ready to use. Stir before serving.

Blueberry Streusel Tea Cake with Blueberry Curd

We look forward each summer to the arrival of the blueberry crop. We drive just a few miles along country roads to pick up our freshly-harvested berries. We fill our freezer and look for any excuse to work the sweet blue treasures into a recipe. This tea cake is one of our favorite blueberry indulgences.

2 cups butter, softened
3 cups sugar
6 eggs
1 cup milk
2 teaspoons lemon extract
1 teaspoon fresh lemon zest
1 tablespoon baking powder
4 cups all-purpose flour
2 cups fresh or frozen blueberries

Grease and flour a 10-inch tube or bundt pan. Preheat oven to 325° F. Cream the butter and sugar with an electric mixer. Add eggs one at a time and mix well. Combine milk and lemon extract in a separate bowl. On low speed, alternately add the wet and dry ingredients. Mix until batter is smooth. Coat blueberries with the remaining cup of flour and gently fold into the batter.

Pour into prepared pan. Sprinkle streusel topping over cake. Bake for one hour. Cool in pan for ten minutes, then turn onto rack and cool completely. Serve with blueberry curd.

<u>Streusel Topping</u>
1/2 cup light brown sugar firmly packed
2 tablespoons soft butter
2 tablespoons all-purpose flour
1 teaspoon cinnamon
1/2 cup chopped almonds (optional)

In a small bowl combine brown sugar, butter, flour, cinnamon and nuts. Mix with fork until crumbly. Set aside until ready to use.

Callie's Christmas Cake

This cake is reminiscent of the Victorian sandwich cake, a staple on the English tea table. The recipe comes from Callie Minks, one of our talented pastry chefs.

Cake
3/4 cup butter, softened
3/4 cup sugar
3 eggs, beaten
1 1/2 cups self-rising flour
4 teaspoons boiling water

Preheat oven to 325° F. Grease two 8-inch round cake pans and line with wax paper. In a large bowl, beat together butter and sugar until light and fluffy. Gradually beat in eggs. Fold in flour. Stir in boiling water to make a soft batter. Divide batter between prepared pans. Bake 25 to 30 minutes or until cakes are lightly browned. Cool in pans five minutes, then turn out. Peel off wax paper liner and transfer to wire rack to cool completely.

Raspberry Curd Filling
3 eggs, beaten
1/2 cup unsalted butter, melted and cooled
1 cup sugar
1/2 cup raspberry puree (fresh or frozen raspberries may be used)

In the top of double boiler, heat eggs until frothy. Stir in melted butter, sugar and raspberry puree. Place over simmering water. Stir constantly for 20 minutes. The mixture should become slightly thickened. Remove from heat and spoon into pint-sized container. Cool to room temperature, cover, and refrigerate for at least two hours before serving.

Frosting
1 cup powdered sugar, sifted
2 teaspoons lemon juice
red food coloring

Mix together powdered sugar, lemon juice, a drop of food coloring, and enough water to make a good consistency for drizzling over cake. To assemble, place one cake on a cake plate. Spread top with Raspberry Curd. Top with second cake. Drizzle frosting in a crisscross pattern.

Chocolate Buttermilk Mocha Pound Cake

You won't find coffee listed on our beverage menu but we do work it into a few recipes. The winning combination of buttermilk, coffee and chocolate makes this rich cake a favorite dessert for our guests. Be sure to cut conservative slices when serving friends for afternoon tea.
They can always ask for more.

1 1/2 cups butter, softened
3 cups sugar
5 eggs
2 teaspoons vanilla
2 teaspoons instant coffee dissolved in 1/4 cup hot water
1 cup buttermilk
2 cups all-purpose flour
3/4 cup unsweetened cocoa
1/2 teaspoon baking powder
1 teaspoon salt

Preheat oven to 325° F. Grease and flour a 10-inch tube pan. In a medium bowl, mix together flour, cocoa, baking powder and salt. Set aside.

In a large mixing bowl, cream together butter and sugar. Beat in eggs one at a time. Stir in vanilla. Beat in flour mixture, alternately with dissolved coffee and buttermilk. Pour into tube pan. Bake 60 to 70 minutes or until toothpick inserted in middle comes out clean.

Carrot-Pineapple Tea Cake

Afternoon teas at Elmwood Inn have always included a cake course. Be sure to cut thin slices if you are serving several courses at your tea. You don't want to satisfy the desire for sweets with just one item.

3 cups flour
2 cups sugar
1 1/2 teaspoons baking soda
2 teaspoons cinnamon
1/2 teaspoon baking powder
1/2 teaspoon salt
1 1/4 cups crushed pineapple
2 cups grated carrots
5 eggs
1/2 cup salad oil
2 teaspoons vanilla

Preheat oven to 325° F. Grease and lightly flour a tube or bundt pan.

Mix together flour, sugar, cinnamon, baking soda, baking powder, and salt. Drain pineapple and reserve juice. Reserve 2-3 tablespoons pineapple juice and add remaining juice to dry mixture. Add eggs, oil, and vanilla. Beat 3 minutes. Stir in pineapple and carrots. Bake at 325° F for 1 1/2 hours. Cool 10 minutes in pan before un-molding.

Glaze
1 1/2 cups powdered sugar
2-3 tablespoons reserved pineapple juice

Mix ingredients together and pour over warm cake.

Chocolate Zucchini Cake

Kentucky gardens overflow with zucchini in late July and August. Our chefs look for recipes to use the bountiful supply. While eating this delicious chocolate tea cake, you will never suspect you're also eating a healthy green vegetable!

3 cups flour
1 1/2 teaspoons baking powder
1 teaspoon baking soda
1 teaspoon salt
4 eggs
3 cups sugar
3 squares baking chocolate, melted and cooled
1 1/2 cups canola oil
2 cups shredded zucchini
powdered sugar for garnish

Preheat oven to 325° F. Grease and flour a 10-inch tube pan. In a medium bowl sift together flour, baking powder, soda and salt. Set aside. In a large mixing bowl, beat eggs and add sugar, 1/4 cup at a time. Add chocolate, then oil.

Add flour mixture and blend well. Fold in zucchini. When blended well, pour into cake pan. Bake for one hour and 15 minutes or until cake tester comes out clean. Cool about 15 minutes before removing cake from pan. Sprinkle with powdered sugar and serve.

Elmwood's Derby Cake

In Kentucky, everything stops the first Saturday in May for the traditional "Run for the Roses" at Louisville's historic Churchill Downs. Here's our contribution to the festivities.

3 cups all-purpose flour
2 teaspoons baking powder
1/2 teaspoon salt
1 cup (2 sticks) butter, softened
1 cup granulated sugar
1 cup light brown sugar, packed
1 1/2 teaspoons vanilla extract
3 eggs
1 cup buttermilk
1 1/2 cups semi-sweet chocolate mini-chips
3/4 cup pecan pieces
1/2 cup coconut (optional)
Kentucky bourbon (optional)

Soak pecan pieces in bourbon until ready to use. Drain before adding to cake batter. Heat oven to 325° F. Grease and flour a 10-inch tube pan. In a medium bowl, stir together flour, baking powder and salt. In a large mixer bowl, beat together butter, granulated sugar, brown sugar, and vanilla until light and fluffy. Add eggs, one at a time, beating well after each addition. Add flour mixture alternately with buttermilk to butter mixture, beating well after each addition. Stir in chocolate chips, pecans, and coconut. Pour into cake pan; bake 55 to 60 minutes, or until wooden pick inserted into cake comes out clean. Cool 15 minutes and remove from pan. Cool completely before glazing.

<u>Glaze</u>
2 tablespoons sugar
2 tablespoons water
1/2 cup semi-sweet chocolate mini-chips

In small sauce pan, combine sugar and water. Heat to boiling and stir until sugar is dissolved. Remove from heat and immediately add chocolate chips. Stir until completely melted and pour over cake.

Harvest Moon Cake with Orange Sauce

This cake has just the right combination of fall colors and tastes to celebrate the season of cool, crisp nights and turning leaves. The easy-to-make sauce sets the plate aglow with brilliant orange hues and aroma.

3 cups all-purpose flour
2 teaspoons baking powder
1 teaspoon baking soda
2 teaspoons cinnamon
1/4 teaspoon ground ginger
1/4 teaspoon ground allspice
4 eggs
1 cup brown sugar, packed
1/3 cup canola oil
1 1/4 cups honey
3/4 cup cold black tea
1/4 cup brandy or orange juice
1/2 cup raisins
1/2 cup dried apricots, cut up
1/2 cup chopped pecans (optional)

Preheat oven to 325° F. Grease and flour a 10-inch tube pan.

Combine dry ingredients and spices. In a mixing bowl, beat eggs, sugar, and oil until light. Add honey and mix well. Add dry ingredients alternately with tea and brandy, ending with dry ingredients. Mix until just blended. Stir in raisins, apricots, and nuts by hand. Pour batter into pan and bake at 325° F for one hour and 15 minutes, or until a cake tester comes out dry. Remove from oven, place on cake rack and cool for 10 minutes. Loosen cake from pan and carefully invert onto serving platter.

<u>Orange Sauce</u>
1 1/2 cups orange marmalade
1/2 cup sugar

In a medium saucepan, combine preserves, sugar, and 1/2 cup water. Bring to a boil over medium heat. Boil, stirring constantly for 5 minutes. Pour over cake and let cool, or serve as a sauce and spoon over cake after cutting.

Irish Cream and Coffee Poundcake

Here is a cake that freezes well and cuts easily - two attributes we often look for in determining a good tea cake. The coffee overtones may be complemented by a strong cup of Irish or Assam tea.

1 1/2 cups butter, softened
3 cups sugar
6 large eggs
1 1/2 tablespoons instant coffee granules
1/4 cup boiling water
1/2 cup Irish Cream liqueur
4 cups all-purpose flour
1 teaspoon vanilla extract
1 teaspoon almond extract
3 tablespoons toasted sliced almonds

Preheat oven to 300° F. Beat butter at medium speed with an electric mixer until soft and creamy. Gradually add sugar, beating at medium speed five to seven minutes. Add eggs, one at a time, beating just until yellow disappears. Dissolve coffee granules in boiling water; stir in liqueur. Add flour to butter mixture alternately with coffee mixture, beginning and ending with coffee mixture. Mix at low speed just until blended after each addition. Stir in extracts.

Pour batter into a greased and floured tube pan. Bake at 300° F for one hour and 40 minutes or until a wooden pick inserted in center comes out clean. Pour glaze over warm (not hot) cake.

Irish Cream Glaze
1 1/2 cups powdered sugar
1/8 cup Irish Cream liqueur

Whisk together and drizzle over cake. More or less Irish Cream may be added to reach desired consistency.

Painted Lady Butterfly Tea Cake

Cake
1 1/2 cups butter, room temperature
3 cups sugar
5 eggs
3 cups all-purpose flour
2 teaspoons lemon extract
3/4 cup lemon-lime soda
1 to 2 drops yellow food color (optional)
1/2 cup pineapple-orange juice
1 cup toasted coconut

Preheat oven to 325° F. Grease and flour a 10-inch tube pan. Cream together butter and sugar, about ten minutes. Add eggs, one at a time, beating well. Add flour and lemon extract. Fold in the lemon-lime soda. Add food color. Pour into prepared cake pan and bake 60 to 75 minutes or until cake tester comes out clean. Cool, then remove from pan. Poke holes in the top and spoon orange-pineapple juice over the top of the cake. Cover with toasted coconut and decorate with iced sugar cookies.

Painted Lady Sugar Cookies
2/3 cup shortening
3/4 cup sugar
1/2 teaspoon vanilla
4 teaspoons milk
2 cups sifted flour
1 1/2 teaspoons baking powder
1/4 teaspoon salt

Preheat oven to 325° F. Cream together shortening, sugar and vanilla. Sift dry ingredients and blend into mixture. Add milk and blend until combined. Chill one hour. Roll to 1/8-inch thickness on floured surface. Using a small butterfly cookie cutter, cut out shapes and place on a parchment-lined cookie sheet. Bake 6 to 8 minutes. Cool slightly, then remove to cool completely on wire rack.

To make a quick icing, mix about four cups of powdered sugar with 3 to 4 tablespoons water. Add more powdered sugar or water to make the desired consistency. Divide into smaller bowls and add the colors desired. Paint the cookies using small brushes.

Strawberry Tea Cake

Strawberries are not just for serving over cake. They are baked into the batter of this scrumptious tea cake. Enhance the presentation with fresh strawberries, sliced or whole, placed on the serving dish.

3 cups all-purpose flour
1 teaspoon baking soda
1 teaspoon salt
1 tablespoon cinnamon
2 cups sugar
4 eggs, beaten
2 cups frozen strawberries, thawed
1 1/2 cups canola oil
1 1/4 cups finely chopped almonds

Glaze
1 cup confectioners' sugar
4 tablespoons pureed strawberries
1/2 teaspoon almond extract

Preheat oven to 325° F. Grease and flour two 9-inch loaf pans. Sift together dry ingredients. Combine eggs, strawberries, and oil. Add to dry ingredients. Add almonds. Bake for about one hour or until cake tester inserted in center comes out dry. Remove from oven. Cool for 10 minutes. Remove from pans and continue to cool for an additional 20 minutes on a rack. Combine the glaze ingredients and drizzle over the cooled loaves.

Chocolate Cherry Christmas Bars

We have served these chocolate brownies with the marvelous middles several times at Christmas. This recipe has been requested over and over again. If you serve it to your guests, be prepared to share the recipe!

4 ounces unsweetened baking chocolate
1 cup butter
2 cups sugar
2 teaspoons vanilla
4 eggs
1 1/2 cups all-purpose flour
1/2 teaspoon salt
1 cup chopped nuts

Cherry Cheese Filling
2 8-ounce packages cream cheese, softened
1/2 cup sugar
1/2 cup chopped red maraschino cherries
2 teaspoons cherry juice
1 egg

Preheat oven to 325° F. Grease a 13x9x2 rectangular pan.

Make the cherry cheese filling by beating all of the ingredients until smooth. Set aside.

Melt the chocolate and butter over low heat, stirring often. Remove from heat and cool. Using an electric mixer on medium speed, beat together chocolate mixture, sugar, vanilla, and eggs for about one minute, scraping the bowl occasionally. Beat in flour and salt. Stir in nuts. Spread half of the batter (about 2 1/2 cups) in the pan. Spread cherry cheese filling over the batter. Carefully spread remaining batter over the filling. Swirl a knife through both batters to create a marbled design.

Chocolate-Covered Cherry Cookies

*We are always looking for cherry recipes for the month of February.
Mr. and Mrs. Rod Huber make the two-hour drive from Cincinnati almost
every month to have tea with us. They shared this recipe that
perfectly fills the bill!*

1 1/2 cups all-purpose flour
1/2 cup unsweetened cocoa powder
1/2 cup butter, softened
1 cup granulated sugar
1/4 teaspoon baking soda
1/4 teaspoon baking powder
1/4 teaspoon salt
1 egg
1 1/2 teaspoons vanilla
48 maraschino cherries, not drained

In a medium bowl, mix flour and cocoa. Set aside. In a large mixing bowl,
beat butter with an electric mixer on medium speed for about 30 seconds.
Add the sugar, baking soda, baking powder, and salt. Beat until combined. Beat in egg and vanilla. Beat in as much of the flour mixture as
possible using the mixer. Stir in by hand any remaining flour mixture.
Shape dough into 1-inch balls. Place 2 inches apart on an ungreased
cookie sheet. Press down center of each ball with thumb. Drain cherries,
reserving juice. Place a cherry in center of each cookie.

Frosting
1 cup semisweet chocolate pieces (6 ounces)
1/2 cup sweetened condensed milk
reserved cherry juice

In a small saucepan, combine chocolate pieces and sweetened
condensed milk. Heat on low until chocolate is melted. Stir in four
teaspoons of reserved cherry juice. Spoon about one teaspoon of frosting
over each cherry, spreading to cover cherry.

Bake in a 325° F oven for about 10 minutes or until sides are set. Transfer
cookies to wire rack and cool. These cookies can be made ahead and
frozen up to three months. Before serving, thaw for 15 minutes.

Elmwood Macaroons

*Children are always looking for a way they can help in the kitchen.
Macaroons are easy to make and children of every age love to eat them
- sometimes before they are completely cooled.*

14 ounces sweetened condensed milk
2 teaspoons vanilla extract
1 1/2 teaspoons almond extract
2 7-ounce packages flaked coconut
1/4 cup flour
2 ounces semisweet chocolate
1/2 teaspoon shortening

Preheat oven to 325° F. Grease and flour a foil-lined pan. In mixing bowl,
combine and mix the sweetened condensed milk, vanilla, and almond
extract. In a separate bowl, combine the coconut and flour. Add the
coconut/flour mixture to milk mixture. Stir together and drop by
teaspoonfuls onto the foil-lined pan. Flatten slightly and bake 15 to 17
minutes. Remove from oven and cool for about 10 minutes. Remove to a
wire rack to cool completely.

To make topping, melt chocolate and shortening in a small heavy
saucepan. Drizzle melted chocolate over cooled cookies. Makes about
3 1/2 dozen.

Chocolate Orange Mousse Tarts

Tarts always make an elegant dessert or tea sweet. The garnish of orange rind lets your guests know they are in for a flavorful treat.

1/2 pound very good quality semi-sweet chocolate
6 tablespoons water
pinch of salt
5 eggs, separated
1 teaspoon pure orange oil
1 tablespoon finely grated orange zest
2 tablespoons orange liqueur
chocolate curls for garnish
orange twists for garnish
prepared tart shells
orange rind strips

Chop chocolate into small pieces and place in double boiler with water and salt. Heat until the chocolate is melted. Cool for two minutes. Very quickly, beat the egg yolks into the chocolate, one at a time. Beat in the extract, zest, and liqueur. Using a clean bowl and clean beaters, whip the egg whites until soft peaks form. Fold gently into the chocolate mixture. Pour into a large bowl and refrigerate over night.

When ready to serve, spoon mixture into individual pastry shells. Garnish with chocolate curls and orange twists. Makes about 48 mini-tarts.

Fruit and Ricotta Tarts

<u>Tart Shells</u>
6 tablespoons butter
3 tablespoons sugar
2 tablespoons egg substitute
1 teaspoon freshly grated lemon peel
1 cup all-purpose flour

Beat together butter, sugar, and egg substitute in a small bowl until well blended. Stir in the lemon peel and flour, blending well to make a soft dough. Wrap dough in plastic wrap and refrigerate one hour.

Preheat oven to 325° F. Press two to three teaspoons of dough over bottom and up sides of 24 two-inch tartlet pans. Place on baking sheet. Bake for 10 to 12 minutes or until golden brown. Cool in pans for five minutes. Remove shells to wire rack to cool completely.

<u>Ricotta Filling</u>
3/4 cup ricotta cheese
1/4 cup confectioners' sugar
2 tablespoons finely chopped mixed candied fruit
1/4 square semi-sweet chocolate, finely chopped
1 tablespoon orange liqueur or extract
an assortment of fresh fruits, such as strawberries,
blueberries, raspberries, kiwi, and orange segments
1/2 cup peach or apricot preserves, heated, thinned, and strained
3 tablespoons chopped pistachio nuts (optional)

Combine ricotta cheese, confectioners' sugar, candied fruit, chocolate, and orange extract in a small bowl. Mix until blended. Cover and refrigerate until ready to use. Fill each tart shell with 1-2 teaspoons ricotta filling. Arrange a mixture of whole or cut-up fruit on top. Brush with preserve glaze. Sprinkle with pistachio nuts and serve immediately.

Makes 24.

Fruited Oatmeal Tea Cakes

1 1/2 cups old-fashioned rolled oats
1 cup flour
3/4 teaspoon salt
1/2 teaspoon baking soda
1/4 teaspoon ground cinnamon
1/2 pound unsalted butter, room temperature
1 cup sugar
1 teaspoon vanilla
1 egg
1/3 cup raisins
1/3 cup chopped dates
1/3 cup chopped dried apricots

Heat oven to 325° F. Butter a 13x9 baking pan. Combine oats, flour, salt, soda, and cinnamon. With an electric mixer set at medium speed, beat butter, sugar, and vanilla until light and fluffy. Beat in egg. Reduce to low speed and beat in oat mixture until just combined. Stir in fruit with a spoon. Spread mixture evenly in pan. Bake until golden brown (35-40 minutes). Cool completely and cut into squares or triangles. Makes 48.

Chocolate Creme de Menthe Bars

Our customers have asked us for this recipe for years. Be sure to make twice as many as you expect to serve because they are irresistible! It will be the dessert your guests ask for again and again.

Brownies
1 cup sugar
1/2 cup butter, softened
1 teaspoon vanilla
2 eggs
2/3 cup all-purpose flour
1/2 cup baking cocoa
1/2 teaspoon salt

Heat oven to 325° F. Grease an 8-inch square pan.

In a medium bowl, beat sugar, 1/2 cup butter, vanilla, and eggs with an electric mixer. In another bowl, combine flour, cocoa, baking powder and salt. Add to the butter mixture, stirring by hand. Spread evenly in pan.

Bake 25 to 30 minutes or until toothpick inserted in the center comes out clean. Cool fifteen minutes.

Mint Layer
3 cups powdered sugar
1/3 cup butter, softened
2 tablespoons green creme de menthe
2 tablespoons creme de cacao

Mix ingredients and spread over brownies. Refrigerate 20 minutes.

Topping
1 1/2 ounces unsweetened baking chocolate

Heat chocolate over low heat until melted. Spread evenly over mint layer. Refrigerate three hours. Cut into bars. Makes about 50.

Snow Bars

This is another of our most requested recipes that will have your guests asking for seconds and thirds.

1/2 cup butter
1 12-ounce package vanilla milk chips
2 eggs
1/2 cup sugar
1 cup flour
1/2 teaspoon salt
1 teaspoon almond extract
1/2 cup raspberry jam
powdered sugar

Heat oven to 325° F. Grease and flour a 9-inch square pan. Melt butter in a small saucepan over low heat. Remove from heat. Add 1 cup of the vanilla milk chips. Do not stir, but allow to stand.

In a large bowl, beat eggs until foamy. Gradually add sugar, beating at high speed until lemon-colored. Stir in the white chocolate mixture. Add flour, salt, and almond extract. Mix at low speed until combined. Spread about 1 cup of batter into pan. Bake at 325° F for 15 to 20 minutes or until light golden brown. Stir remaining 1 cup vanilla milk chips into remaining half of batter. Set aside.

Melt the jam in a small saucepan over low heat. Spread evenly over warm, partially baked crust. Spoon teaspoonfuls of remaining batter over jam and ease together to create top layer. It is okay if some jam shows through.

Return to oven and bake an additional 25 to 30 minutes or until a toothpick inserted into the center comes out clean. Cool and cut into bars. Dust with powdered sugar.

Elmwood Lemon Squares

Lemon squares are common items on many tea trays, but there is nothing "common" about this recipe. These rich, buttery bars are the perfect blend of sweet and tart. Keep them refrigerated, but let sit at room temperature for half an hour before serving.

1 1/2 cups unbleached all-purpose flour
1 teaspoon baking powder
1/2 teaspoon salt
1 15-ounce can sweetened condensed milk
1/4 teaspoon lemon oil
1/2 cup lemon juice
5 1/3 ounces butter
1 cup dark brown sugar, firmly packed
1 cup old-fashioned or quick-cooking oats

Preheat oven to 325° F. Sift together the flour, baking powder, and salt. Set aside.

Combine the condensed milk, lemon oil and juice in a medium-sized mixing bowl. Stir with a wire whisk until smooth. Mixture will thicken. Set aside.

In a large bowl, cream the butter and sugar. Add the sifted ingredients, then the oats; mixture will be crumbly. Pat two cups of crumbs into bottom of a greased 9x13-inch pan. Spread condensed milk mixture atop crumb layer; sprinkle remaining crumb mixture over milk layer, smoothing gently.

Bake at 325° F for 30 to 35 minutes, or until bars are brown around edges. Remove pan from oven and cool completely. Cut into small squares when completely cool, then refrigerate. Let them come to room temperature before serving. Makes about 30 bars.

Iced Cinnamon Apple Oatmeal Tea Cookies

2 cups brown sugar, packed
1 cup butter, softened
2 eggs
1 teaspoon vanilla
2 1/4 cups all-purpose flour
2 cups old-fashioned oatmeal
1 teaspoon baking powder
1 teaspoon freshly grated nutmeg
1 teaspoon cinnamon
1/2 teaspoon baking soda
1/4 teaspoon salt
1 1/2 cups peeled and finely diced Granny Smith apples
1 cup raisins
1 cup chopped walnuts

Preheat oven to 325° F. Beat brown sugar and butter together with an electric mixer on medium speed until light and fluffy. Beat in eggs one at a time until well-blended. Add vanilla and mix well.

Mix together flour, oatmeal, baking powder, nutmeg, cinnamon, baking soda, and salt. Add to butter mixture and beat until well-blended. Stir in apples, raisins, and walnuts. Drop by teaspoonfuls onto a greased cookie sheet. Bake 15 to 18 minutes or until the edges just begin to brown. Remove from oven and cool on cookie sheets two to three minutes. Remove to wire rack and cool completely.

Icing
3 cups confectioners' sugar
1/2 teaspoon cinnamon
1/4 cup apple cider (or just enough to make a thick, pourable icing)

Stir together the sugar, cinnamon, and cider. Drizzle icing over each cookie, then allow to dry. Makes about 40 cookies.

Orange Coconut Sorbet

2 quarts freshly squeezed orange juice
1 cup simple syrup (page 128)
1/2 cup cream of coconut
1/2 cup coconut

Mix all ingredients together in a large bowl. Freeze in a sorbet maker or in the freezer by pouring mixture into an aluminum bowl and stirring at intervals until firm.

Gingerbread Scones

2 cups all-purpose flour
2 teaspoons baking powder
1/2 teaspoon salt
1/4 teaspoon baking soda
1/3 cup dark brown sugar, packed
3/4 teaspoon ground cinnamon
1/2 teaspoon ground ginger
1/8 teaspoon ground cloves
6 tablespoons unsalted butter
2/3 cup currants
1/2 cup buttermilk
1 egg
1 teaspoon vanilla
1 egg white, slightly whisked

Preheat oven to 400° F. Lightly grease a large baking sheet. In a large mixing bowl combine flour, baking powder, salt, baking soda, brown sugar, cinnamon, ginger, and cloves. With a pastry blender, cut in butter until the mixture resembles coarse crumbs. Mix in currants.

Whisk buttermilk, egg and vanilla together. Pour into dry mixture. Stir together quickly until a soft dough forms. Turn onto a lightly floured surface and turn over 5 to 6 times. Roll the dough with a floured rolling pin to about 1/2-inch thickness. Using a round cutter, cut scones out and place on baking sheet. Brush the tops with egg white. Bake 10 to 12 minutes or until lightly browned. Serve with lemon curd. Makes 12 scones. Scones are pictured on page 16.

Watermelon Sorbet

On a warm summer afternoon, you will often find our kitchen staff enjoying this refreshing sorbet. It is their favorite.

1 small seedless watermelon
simple syrup (page 128)

Cut watermelon in half. Scoop out flesh and place in a large bowl. Save the outer rind if desired to use for a natural bowl.

Place watermelon in a blender and add only enough simple syrup to make a thick mushy mixture. Pour into an aluminum bowl and place in freezer. Stir mixture at intervals until a thick frozen mush is formed. Allow to freeze completely. When ready to serve, scoop into balls and garnish with fresh mint or lemon balm.

Chocolate Mousse Halloween Tarts

1 cup whipping cream, divided
1 egg yolk
2 tablespoons corn syrup
2 tablespoons butter
4 squares semisweet chocolate, chopped
4 squares milk chocolate, chopped
5 teaspoons powdered sugar
1/2 teaspoon vanilla
candy corn for garnish

Whisk together 1/2 cup whipping cream, egg yolk, corn syrup, and butter in a heavy saucepan over medium heat. Continue whipping until mixture simmers for two minutes. Remove from heat. Add chocolates, stirring until smooth. Cool.

In a medium bowl, beat remaining 1/2 cup cream with electric mixer at high speed until soft peaks form. Add powdered sugar and vanilla. Beat until stiff peaks form. Stir whipped cream into chocolate mixture. Spoon or pipe mixture into prepared pastry cups. Garnish with candy corn and chill two to four hours. Tarts are pictured on page 136.

Frozen Passion Sorbet

The last course in our afternoon tea is usually a beautiful, light scoop of sorbet. Not too heavy, it adds a flavorful final note to a symphony of sights and tastes.

2 14-ounce cans sweetened condensed milk
1 46-ounce can pineapple juice, chilled
8 ounces cream of coconut
12 ounces partially thawed sweetened strawberries

In a large aluminum bowl, combine all ingredients. Make sure the strawberries are evenly distributed. Freeze to a firm mush (one to two hours). Stir, then allow to freeze one hour more. Stir once again, then let freeze until firm.

Use an ice cream scoop to form balls and serve.

Ginger Pear Sorbet

Sorbets are inexpensive and so easy to make. This recipe can be made in either an ice cream or sorbet maker. This recipe is pictured on page 118.

1 15-ounce can pear halves in heavy syrup
1/4 cup simple syrup (page 128)
1 tablespoon finely chopped crystallized ginger
1 teaspoon grated lemon zest
fresh mint leaves for garnish

Combine all ingredients in a blender or food processor. Blend until mixture is pourable. Pour into an aluminum bowl and begin freezing. About two hours later, stir thoroughly, then let mixture freeze completely. When ready to serve, scoop into sorbet dishes and garnish with mint leaves.

End of the Rainbow Sorbet

<u>Strawberry</u>
4 cups fresh strawberries
2/3 cup boiling water
1/2 cup sugar
1 tablespoon lemon juice
2 tablespoons orange juice

In a medium bowl, combine boiling water and sugar. Stir until sugar is dissolved. Cool. Combine strawberries, lemon juice, orange juice, and sugar water in a blender or food processor. Pour into aluminum bowl and place in freezer. After 1 1/2 hours, stir, then continue to freeze, stirring periodically until sorbet becomes a firm mush. Freeze until firm.

<u>Orange</u>
2 cups fresh orange juice
1 1/2 cups boiling water
1/2 cup sugar
2 teaspoons orange zest

Combine boiling water and sugar, stirring until sugar dissolves. Cool. Add orange juice and zest. Pour into an aluminum bowl and place in freezer. After 1 1/2 hours, stir, then continue freezing, stirring periodically until sorbet becomes a firm mush. Freeze until firm.

<u>Lime</u>
3 cups boiling water
1 cup sugar
1 cup fresh lime juice
2 teaspoons lime zest

Combine boiling water and sugar, stirring until sugar dissolves. Cool. Add lime juice and zest. Pour mixture into aluminum bowl and place in freezer, stirring periodically until sorbet becomes a firm mush. Freeze until firm.

<u>For Rainbow Sorbet</u>
With the same ice cream scoop, scoop out a little of each sorbet until the scoop is full. Place in a dish. All three colors will come together.

Mint Julep Sorbet

The favorite drink at the Kentucky Derby is the mint julep. This icy version adds a refreshing hint of lemon.

3 cups simple syrup
juice from 3 lemons
5 tablespoons fresh mint, finely chopped
1/4 cup bourbon (optional)
fresh mint leaves for garnish

Simple syrup recipe: In a large sauce pan, combine 2 cups sugar and 4 cups water. Bring to a boil while stirring. Refrigerate until ready to use.

Pour 3 cups simple syrup, lemon juice and mint into a blender. Blend together for 10 seconds. Add the bourbon if desired and blend again for 5 seconds. Pour mixture into an aluminum bowl and place in freezer. After the mixture begins to become icy, stir. Stir at least twice more, scraping around the edges, until mixture is thick enough to freeze completely. When ready to serve, use an ice cream scoop and mound into julep cups. Garnish with fresh mint leaves.

Petite White Chocolate Mousse Tarts

Pastry Cups
1 cup semi-sweet chocolate chips
1 tablespoon solid vegetable shortening
1 package small pre-baked filo pastry shells (approximately 24)

In small microwave-safe bowl, combine chocolate chips and shortening.
Microwave on HIGH one minute; stir until melted and smooth. Microwave
an additional 30 seconds, if needed. Tilt the bowl slightly; dip top edge of
filo cups into melted chocolate. (There will be leftover chocolate.) Set
aside on serving plate until chocolate is firm.

White Chocolate Mousse
8 1-ounce squares white baking chocolate, chopped
2 tablespoons milk
1 tablespoon orange extract
2 teaspoons grated orange peel
8 ounces whipped topping

In a large microwave-safe bowl, combine white baking chocolate, milk,
and orange extract. Microwave on HIGH power one minute; stir the
chocolate mixture until melted and smooth. Microwave an additional 30
seconds, if needed. Cool to room temperature (about 15 minutes). Stir in
grated orange peel. Fold whipped topping into the cooled white chocolate
mixture. Gently spoon mousse into a large pastry bag fitted with a star
tip. Pipe mousse into each pastry cup just until it reaches the top of the
cup. Refrigerate for one hour or overnight.

Optional Garnishes
To make chocolate shapes for garnish, line a baking sheet with waxed
paper. Spoon some of the remaining melted chocolate into a small plastic
bag. Snip small tip from one corner of the bag; pipe chocolate onto the
waxed paper into desired shapes. Let stand until chocolate is firm and
shapes are solid. As an alternative, sprinkle mousse with crushed toffee.

Raspberry and Cardamon Cake Trifle

<u>Custard</u>
1 cup sugar
1 tablespoon cornstarch
1/2 teaspoon salt
4 cups milk
8 egg yolks
2 teaspoons vanilla extract

In a heavy saucepan, combine sugar, cornstarch, and salt. Add milk. Cook over medium heat, stirring constantly until mixture comes to a boil and begins to thicken. Boil 1 minute, then remove from heat. In a medium bowl, beat egg yolks slightly. Add a little of the hot milk mixture to the eggs. Keep stirring until all eggs are incorporated. Cook over medium heat stirring constantly until mixture boils. Remove from heat and stir in vanilla. Pour into bowl, cover with plastic wrap, and refrigerate.

<u>Cardamon Cake</u>
2 eggs, separated
2 1/4 cups sifted cake flour
1 teaspoon baking powder
1 teaspoon baking soda
1 1/2 teaspoons cardamon
3/4 cup sugar
3/4 cup honey
3/4 cup orange juice
3/4 cup toasted macadamia nuts, chopped
2 tablespoons sugar
4-5 cups fresh or frozen raspberries

Preheat oven to 325° F. Grease and lightly flour a 10-inch tube pan. Sift cake flour, baking powder, baking soda, and cardamon into a small mixing bowl. Heat butter over low heat in a small saucepan until melted. Continue heating until butter turns a delicate brown. Pour into a large mixing bowl. Add egg yolks, sugar, and honey. Beat with an electric mixer on medium speed until combined. Add flour mixture alternately with the orange juice, beating on low speed after each addition until combined. Fold in macadamia nuts. Beat egg whites and 2 tablespoons sugar in a medium mixing bowl until stiff peaks form. Fold whites into batter. Spoon batter into prepared pan. Bake for 35 minutes or until a wooden toothpick inserted near the center comes out clean. Cool in pan for 10 minutes and cut into cubes. Assemble trifle by layering custard, cake, and berries. Top with whipped cream and mint.

Kentucky Christmas Balls

One bite of this delicious truffle will remind you very quickly of the beverage that makes Kentucky famous.

1 12-ounce box vanilla wafers
1 cup walnuts, toasted lightly
1 cup powdered sugar
1/2 cup semisweet chocolate chips, melted
1/4 cup white corn syrup
1/4 cup Kentucky bourbon

In a food processor, crush the vanilla wafers and walnuts. Pour into a large bowl and add next five ingredients. Stir well. If the batter appears dry, add a little more corn syrup. Shape into 1-inch balls. Refrigerate until ready to serve. Roll in additional powdered sugar and arrange festively. Makes about 5 dozen.

Chocolate Hazelnut Truffles

This recipe comes to us from Monica Miller, our tea friend and founder of the American Tea Society.

8 ounces bittersweet chocolate, chopped
1/4 cup Nutella hazelnut spread
3 tablespoons heavy cream
1/2 cup hazelnuts, skinned and chopped

Microwave chocolate until nearly melted, about 60-90 seconds. Remove from microwave and stir until smooth. Stir in Nutella until smooth. Stir in cream. The mixture will thicken almost immediately. Refrigerate, stirring once or twice, until it has cooled and thickened to a truffle consistency. This will only take about 5-10 minutes.

In food processor, pulse the hazelnuts once or twice until finely chopped. Place on a plate or shallow dish. Pinch off and form the truffle mixture into walnut-size balls. Roll each truffle in the nuts to coat. Let truffles dry on a piece of waxed paper for at least five minutes. The truffles can be refrigerated (tightly covered) for up to five days or frozen for one month. Serve at room temperature. Makes about 24 truffles.

Key Lime Coconut Truffles

If you like Key Lime Pie, you will love these bite-size morsels enhanced with coconut.

5 cups sweetened, shredded coconut
1 14-ounce can sweetened condensed milk (fat free)
1/3 cup light corn syrup
1 tablespoon vanilla extract
3 tablespoons key lime juice
1 teaspoon grated key lime zest
1/2 cup graham cracker crumbs
1 pound confectioners' sugar
1 to 2 drops green food coloring (optional)

Preheat oven to 325° F. Spread 2 cups coconut on a baking sheet and bake for 5 to 7 minutes or until lightly toasted, tossing once or twice during baking. Remove from oven and transfer to a bowl to cool.

In a large bowl, combine three cups coconut, condensed milk, corn syrup, vanilla, key lime juice, zest, and graham crackers. Add the confectioners' sugar and food coloring. Beat until combined thoroughly. Place mixture in refrigerator until cold. Form 1-inch balls from the chilled mixture, then generously roll in toasted coconut. Place in freezer before serving or wrap tightly and store in freezer for up to one month.

Raspberry Truffles

1 8-ounce package cream cheese, softened
1 6-ounce package semisweet chocolate chips, melted
3/4 cup vanilla wafer crumbs
1/4 cup seedless raspberry preserves
1/2 cup almonds, toasted and finely chopped
2 tablespoons Chambord (optional)

Beat cream cheese with an electric mixer until creamy. Add the chocolate and beat until smooth. Stir in vanilla wafer crumbs, preserves, and Chambord. Cover and chill one hour. Shape into 1 inch balls, roll in chopped almonds, and chill until ready to serve. May also be frozen.

Sticky Toffee Tea Cookies

Traditional sticky toffee pudding is one of our favorite English recipes. This toffee cookie is flat and airy, similar to a lace cookie.

7 1-ounce English toffee candy bars
3/4 cup flour
3/4 cup old-fashioned oatmeal
1/2 teaspoon salt
1/2 teaspoon baking soda
6 tablespoons light brown sugar
6 tablespoons white sugar
1 1/2 teaspoons vanilla
1 egg
5 tablespoons butter
5 tablespoons solid shortening

Preheat oven to 325° F. Lightly grease a cookie sheet.

Break candy bars and chop into coarse pieces. In a medium bowl, combine the flour, oatmeal, salt, and baking soda. Add the chopped candy and set aside.

In a large mixing bowl, mix brown sugar, white sugar, vanilla, and egg. Add butter and shortening and mix well. Add the candy/flour mixture and blend well.

Drop by tablespoonfuls one inch apart on the prepared cookie sheet. Bake 8 to 10 minutes or until golden. Remove from oven and cool on wire rack. Makes about 36.

Strawberries with Mascarpone

These colorful creations - sweet, creamy, and crunchy - are a refreshing kiss of spring. We use wild violet leaves from our garden for a highlight.

20 large strawberries
8 ounces Italian mascarpone cheese
1/3 cup superfine sugar
1/2 teaspoon cinnamon
1 tablespoon finely chopped pistachio nuts
fresh violets for garnish

Wash and dry strawberries. Cut berries lengthwise, just above the stem, without damaging the leaves. In a small mixing bowl, combine mascarpone, sugar, and cinnamon. Stir with a spoon until mixture is creamy and smooth. Transfer to a pastry bag fitted with a star tip. Pipe mixture into each strawberry half. Sprinkle with chopped pistachios and garnish with fresh violet petals. Refrigerate until ready to serve.

Rosemary Shortbread

Pungent rosemary with its piney mint flavor makes a bold addition to traditional sweet shortbread.

1/2 cup unsalted butter, softened
1/3 cup sugar
1/4 teaspoon salt
1 teaspoon vanilla extract
1 cup all purpose flour
1 tablespoon freshly chopped rosemary

Preheat oven to 325° F. In a large bowl, beat sugar and butter until light and fluffy. Add salt and vanilla extract, mixing well. Add flour and rosemary, stirring until well-combined. Roll out on a floured board to 1/4 inch thickness. Cut out with a cookie cutter. Place cookies on an ungreased cookie sheet and bake for 15-20 minutes.

Cookies should not overbake and should not brown. Cool after removing from oven. This recipe could also be baked in an 8-inch round mold for 45 minutes at 300° F. After removing from oven and cooling, cut into 8 wedges.

Sweet Summer Iced Tea

Our guests sometimes ask for iced tea in the summer. This is a sweetened southern version that is great for picnics.

5 black tea bags
1/4 cup fresh mint leaves
4 cups boiling water
1 cup sugar
6 ounces frozen lemonade concentrate
5 cups water
ice
lemon slices

Steep teabags and mint leaves for about 15 minutes in boiling water. Discard teabags and mint. Add lemonade concentrate, sugar, and remaining water. Mix well and serve over ice. Garnish with lemon slices and fresh mint.

INDEX OF RECIPES

The Benjamin Press staff includes (left to right): Peggy Powell, pastry chef; Ben Richardson, photo editor; Mary Lou Mayes, pastry chef; Shelley Richardson, writer; Jan Sheffield, copy editor; Bruce Richardson, photographer; Freear Williams, editor; and Masha Popkhadze, stylist. Not pictured: Callie Minks, pastry chef.